THE TITANIC

The Maritime Tragedy
that Sank the Unsinkable

Written by Romain Parmentier
In collaboration with Christelle Klein-Scholz
Translated by Carly Probert

History 50MINUTES.com

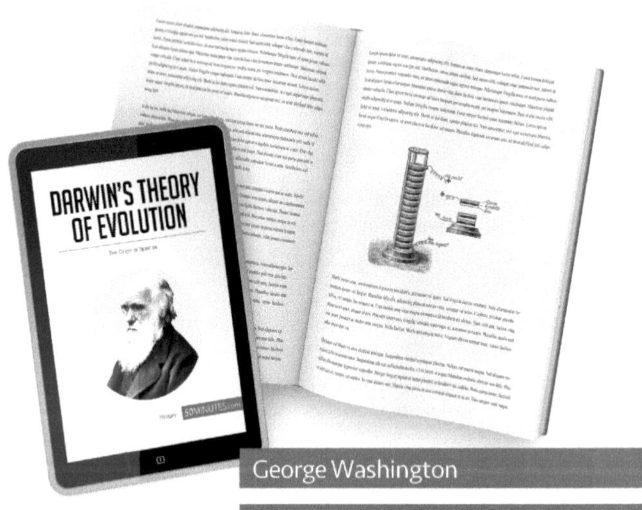

50MINUTES.com

BECOME AN EXPERT
IN HISTORY

George Washington

The Battle of Austerlitz

Neil Armstrong

The Six-Day War

The Fall of Constantinople

www.50minutes.com

THE TITANIC

KEY INFORMATION

- **When:** On the night of 14-15 April 1912
- **Where:** In the Northwest Atlantic
- **Context:** The *Belle Époque* (the era of liner ships)
- **Main actors:**
    - Edward John Smith, British sailor (1850-1912)
    - Thomas Andrews, British naval architect (1873-1912)
    - Joseph Bruce Ismay, British businessman (1862-1937)
- **Repercussions:**
    - New legislation on maritime safety
    - The creation of the International Ice Patrol
    - The birth of a myth surrounding the Titanic

Gigantic, luxurious, beautiful, unsinkable; ever since its creation, the *Titanic* has been the subject of the most beautiful descriptions. For travelers of the early 20th century, there was no doubt about it: the ship, a masterpiece of its industry, was indeed the largest liner in the world. The jewel of the shipping company White Star Line, the *Titanic* was designed, through its luxuriousness and more advanced technology, to far outshine the ships of rival companies in the transatlantic crossing, which connected the Old Continent to New York.

On 10 April 1912, the ship began its maiden voyage, under the command of Edward John Smith, a veteran of the seas who had great confidence in the ship's abilities. 2 200 passengers and crew members were onboard, including some of the biggest celebrities of the time. They all anticipated taking the journey of their dreams, unaware that the prestigious ship was doomed.

On 14 April 1912, sailing at an ever-increasing speed, the *Titanic* headed towards a zone of drifting ice. Although messages of caution continued to warn of the danger looming on the horizon, none of them were really taken into account. But, at 11:40pm, lookouts noticed that the ship was racing towards an iceberg. Despite the quick response of the crew, the starboard side of the *Titanic* struck the ice. The damage was heavy and there were only 1 178 seats available in the lifeboats. One of the worst maritime tragedies in history was about to take place.

CONTEXT

EUROPE: MASTER OF THE WORLD

The *Titanic* alone certainly could not summarize the context of its time. Nevertheless, many similarities can be drawn between the fate of the luxury liner and the coming doom of European society, which was about to be destroyed by the iceberg that was the Great War (1914-1918). Like the ship, the Europe of the late 19th century and early 20th century really was the master of the world. Within a few decades (1830-1870), its economy had been transformed forever by the first industrial revolution (iron, coal and the steam engine). As the first was so successful, a second revolution inaugurating the era of oil, steel and electricity began in 1896. Capitalism became king on the Old Continent, which, following these great changes, saw its population double in just 50 years.

This incredible economic and population growth led Europe to turn to the rest of the world. Indeed, the Old Continent no longer had the food resources or the raw materials needed for its growth. Therefore, it was essential to seek new markets that would provide it with resources, but also consumers. This context thus opened Europe to colonialism and imperialism. Africa and Asia were the victims of this new colonization, which saw the European powers arguing over each plot of land. In 1900, the Old Continent truly dominated the world with its colonies, so much so that one in four people in the world lived in a territory belonging to Britain. Only the United States and Japan managed to escape this hegemony.

After this process of expansion, Europe submitted the rest of the world by imposing its values, its policies and its industry. To the detriment of the colonized peoples, it monopolized all the wealth and redistributed its products, inexorably increasing its own profits. The world was now organized by Europe and for Europe. However, the continuous search for riches created inequalities and divisions between the European nations, to the point where a war seemed inevitable.

THE EFFERVESCENCE OF THE *BELLE ÉPOQUE*

Driven by the innovations in energy and technology, the various industrialized countries were developing a culture of progress in the late 19th and early 20th centuries, encouraging inventors and engineers to constantly push the limits of possibility. The men of the *Belle Époque* showed unrivaled optimism towards science and technology, which, with each step forward, enhanced everyday life for an even brighter future.

The "electricity fairy", created by the invention of the incandescent light bulb by Thomas Edison (American inventor, 1847-1931) in 1879, made its appearance in the big cities, accompanied by the dynamo. Similarly, the first household appliances, such as electric polishers, or the first telephones by Graham Bell (American inventor and physicist, 1847-1922) emerged in the late 19th century. The art of entertainment was no exception, with the invention of the phonograph and the cinema. Finally, science in general, particularly medicine, made great progress with the theory of relativity of

Albert Einstein (American physicist, 1879-1955), discoveries on radioactivity by Marie Curie (French physicist, 1867-1934) and in the field of X-rays and pharmaceuticals. Hygiene became essential for medicine, and the use of chloroform now allowed for general anesthesia.

Thomas Edison and his photographer, 1878.

Therefore, all areas of society underwent changes thanks to the progress of the *Belle Époque*. However, there was one specific phenomenon to which all energy sources would contribute: the abolition of distance.

THE GLORY DAYS OF LINER SHIPS

In this buzzing world, engineers competed to create ever faster transport, with maximum capacity. Indeed, the incredible economic growth of the 19th century pushed manufacturers to send goods, but also information and men around the world as quickly as possible. From the 1830s, the railway network was extended to connect even the remotest regions. Trams then took over in cities that had electricity. The car also appeared at the end of the century, and with the invention of the assembly line, symbolized by the Ford Model T of industrialist Henry Ford (1863-1947), it became one of the first objects of mass consumption. Finally, aviation was in its infancy with the invention of the motorized airplane by the brothers Orville Wright (1871-1948) and Wilbur Wright (1867-1912).

Ford Model T, 1910.

However, these means of transport were not yet sufficiently developed to connect the four corners of the world. In this area, the sea remained the most effective. The great clippers with sails had now been succeeded by huge ships that were capable of carrying thousands of goods and passengers – whether wealthy, servants of simple immigrants. A symbol of industrial strength, the liners were also the result of a fierce rivalry between businessmen, aiming to produce the most luxurious, largest and fastest ships. An award known as the blue ribbon was even awarded to the fastest ship, proof of the competition being waged by ship-owners. In the first half of the 19th century, the first shipping companies opened up the transatlantic route, with the most prestigious being none other than the line connecting the

Old Continent with New York. In the early 20th century, no fewer than 150 ships ensured this junction. With a length of up to 200 meters, their speed now reached 23 knots (about 40km per hour), reducing the crossing to just six days.

It was in this context that the White Star Line company, founded in 1840, launched the project to build the largest and most luxurious ship the world had ever known in 1907. A symbol of the mentality of the time and its prestige, the ship was to be named the RMS *Titanic*.

BIOGRAPHIES

EDWARD JOHN SMITH, SEA VETERAN

Edward John Smith, 1912.

The most experienced navigator of his time in the North Atlantic, Edward John Smith was the captain of the *Titanic* on its maiden voyage. Born in Hanley, England on 27 January 1850, he developed a passion for sailing very early in life and left school at the age of 13 to join the maritime world. First serving as a cabin boy on ships, he obtained his captain's certificate in 1875. Five years later, the young man joined the White Star Line.

In 1887, Edward John Smith was given his first command. In total, no fewer than 17 ships sailed under his command. Given his experience at sea, the captain was appointed commander of the White Star Line fleet in 1904. He then systematically performed the inaugural trips of new ships. Moreover, his passengers liked his calm and reassuring manner, so much so that some wished to travel only with him. The captain's career was indeed almost flawless, with the exception of his journey on the *Olympic* in 1911, during which the ship collided with the *Hawke* cruiser of the Royal Navy. However, this incident did not sully his reputation at all and, in April 1912, he was naturally chosen to command the *Titanic*.

On 10 April, when departing, the commander narrowly avoided a collision with the *New York* liner, which had been drawn in by the mass of the *Titanic* upon its leaving the harbor. The rest of the trip was uneventful, until the evening of Sunday 14 April. Having officiated Mass and spent time with the passengers, he went to rest in his cabin, asking to be woken up in the case of a problem. But, at 11:40pm, the *Titanic* hit an iceberg. Faced with the inevitable sinking of the ocean liner, Edward John Smith ordered the sending of distress signals and the evacuation of the ship. At around 2:00am, the captain gave his final order by freeing the radio operators. What happened to him after this no one knows, except that he is now resting alongside the *Titanic*.

THOMAS ANDREWS, THE SHIPBUILDER

Born on 7 February 1873 in Comber, Ireland, Thomas Andrews was a renowned naval architect, and the designer of the *Titanic*. Fascinated by ships, he left school at the age of 16, in 1889, and became an apprentice in the Harland & Wolff shipyards of his uncle, Lord William Pirrie (Irish businessman, 1847-1924). Receiving no special treatment, the young man ascended through the various departments of the site, until finally achieving the role of designer. It was in this department that he proved himself and realized his true calling. Once he had completed his training period, he climbed the ladder by making many plans for shipping companies, including the White Star Line, and ended up becoming the general director of the construction sites in 1905.

As the company was tasked with the construction of the *Titanic*, Thomas Andrews became its architect and oversaw its construction, from the engine room to the first-class cabins. On 10 April 1912, he participated in the ship's first trip. Accompanied by the project's security group, the architect was indeed responsible for ensuring the smooth operation of the ship and identifying any imperfections. Throughout the journey, he tirelessly scoured the *Titanic* looking for any changes that should be made.

When the ship hit the iceberg, Thomas Andrews was in his cabin. However, the captain immediately informed him of the situation and they left to assess the damage together.

Discovering that five compartments of the *Titanic* were flooded, the architect was the first to realize that the ship was lost and immediately suggested that the passengers be evacuated. During the ship's final hours, Thomas Andrews was constantly helping travelers by sending them in the direction of the lifeboats, showing an exemplary attitude. He was seen for the last time in the first-class smoking room, thoughtfully waiting for the inevitable.

JOSEPH BRUCE ISMAY, SPONSOR

Joseph Bruce Ismay, 1912.

A businessman and the president of the White Star Line, Joseph Bruce Ismay was born on 12 December 1862 in Crosby, England and was the man behind the construction of the *Titanic*. The son of Thomas Henry Ismay (1837-1899), the founder of the company, he naturally followed in his father's footsteps. After his schooling, the young man became an apprentice at the White State Line for four years. Once his training was completed, he continued to work there and succeeded his father in 1899 as the company's head.

Following the tradition of his predecessor, Joseph Bruce Ismay favored the construction of giant, luxurious and safe ships. In 1907, he decided to build three new vessels, called the *Olympic*-class liners (*Olympic*, *Titanic*, and *Gigantic*, which was eventually renamed *Britannic*). On these ships, he refused to add more lifeboats than those required according to legal quotas in order to avoid scaring passengers.

As president of the company, he also participated in the voyage of the *Titanic*. When it sank, the businessman did his best to evacuate passengers and finally climbed into a lifeboat himself. His survival earned him much criticism, but as there was not enough incriminating evidence against him, he did not become the object of a legal investigation. However, he was divested of the presidency of White Star Line.

He died on 15 October 1937 in London.

THE *TITANIC'S* UNIQUE JOURNEY

DELUSIONS OF GRANDEUR

At the beginning of the 20th century, there was stiff competition between the shipping companies. In 1907, the British company Cunard Line launched two super-liners, *Lusitania* (weighing 31 550 tons) and *Mauretania* (weighing 31 938 tons), which became the largest and fastest ships in the world. Faced with this new advancement in gigantism, the White Star Line intended to take up the challenge and immediately piloted the construction of three enormous ships to surpass those of competitor companies, not just on the level of speed, but also in terms of grandeur, luxury and safety. One of those ships was the *Titanic*.

Construction of the ship began on 31 March 1909 in the Harland & Wolff shipyards in Belfast. The work advanced rapidly and in just over two years, the hull made of 2 000 steel sheet plates and more than three million rivets was completed. At the cutting edge of modernity, it had a double bottom and, more importantly, was divided into 16 compartments separated by bulkheads, leading everyone to believe that it was unsinkable. The arming and development work was completed in March 1912. After three years of work, the *Titanic* indeed seemed to be the most gigantic ship ever built, floating at 269.10 meters in length, 28.19 meters wide and weighing 46 329 tons.

But what struck imaginations most of all at that time was the luxuriousness and comfort that prevailed inside the ship. The first-class passengers had real apartments that rivaled those of the best hotel suites, with all the necessary amenities and decorated in different styles, ranging from the Renaissance to the Empire style. They also had access to beautiful promenade decks and a sumptuous staircase crowned by a glass dome that led to several levels of the ship. In addition, although in smaller cabins or dorms the second and third classes were no exception and possessed a level of comfort that far surpassed the first and second classes of other ships. Each class had its own dining room served by excellent restaurants, as well as smoking rooms, lounges and libraries. The ship also had its own gyms, a swimming pool and Turkish baths.

The ship was also at the forefront of technology as it had a remarkable electrical system, rivaling the electricity power plants of many cities, in order to power lights, radiators, telephones and elevators. Similarly, the ship was intended to be as safe as possible with its own Marconi wireless telegraphy station. The only downside was that the ship had only 16 lifeboats and 4 collapsible boats for a total of 1 178 passengers.

Finally, this true floating city had more than 890 crew members, including 66 deckhands, 69 restaurant employees, 325 engineers and 431 people in charge of passenger care. On 2 April 1912, the *Titanic* received its seaworthiness certificate after successfully completing its first sea trials. The super-liner was officially ready for its maiden voyage.

NOTHING BUT THE OCEAN AS FAR AS THE EYE CAN SEE

Titanic's departure from Southampton, 10 of April 1912.

On Wednesday 10 April 1912, the *Titanic* sailed from Southampton (southern England). At noon, the whistles sounded and, under the acclamation of hundreds of people, the ship began to move, pulled by five tugs. But the super-ship had barely begun its journey when it struck danger. Leaving the port, the *Titanic* passed two other ships moored in tandem: the *Oceanic* and the *New York*. The mass of water displaced by the *Titanic* was such that the *New York* was literally sucked in by the giant vessel, to the point of breaking its moorings, and saw its stern drift towards the brand new liner. Fortunately, just when everyone believed that a collision was unavoidable, the captain ordered the engines to stop and a tug managed to recover the mooring of the *New York*, preventing a collision by less than a meter. For many, however, this incident was a bad omen.

Although the departure was delayed by an hour, the *Titanic* still had to make two stops before starting its journey, in order to board new passengers. The first stop was in Cherbourg (France). The imposing size of the ship, which arrived at 6:35pm, prevented it from entering the port, the quays of which were too small. Two White Star Lines ferries were responsible for allowing 22 passengers to disembark and escorting a further 274 to the *Titanic*. Ninety minutes after arriving in Cherbourg, the ship resumed its journey, this time towards Queenstown (Ireland), where it arrived the following day at 11:00am. Once again, the ship was forced to anchor offshore and ferries were used to allow 8 passengers to disembark and 120 to board.

After these two stops, the *Titanic* had 1 317 passengers on board. This still meant that the ship was half empty, as it could accommodate up to 2 604 people. However, this was a common occurrence at the time. For travelers, the running of a new ship inevitably involved some technical difficulties and staff that were not yet accustomed to the new facilities. Nonetheless, the ship boasted real celebrities on board, such as John Jacob Astor IV (1864-1912), a man who became incredibly wealthy through his financial and real estate empire, Benjamin Guggenheim (1865-1912), the American mining tycoon, Lucy Duff Gordon (1863-1935), a renowned English stylist, and Margaret Brown (1867-1932), who had recently become a millionaire.

At 1:30pm, the *Titanic* was finally ready for its great crossing and gradually sailed away from the coast of Ireland, with nothing ahead but the open sea. Those on board had no idea that some of them would never see land again. But for now, the passengers could not wish for better travel conditions.

ICEBERG RIGHT AHEAD!

The *Titanic* sailed perfectly. At least, that is what Thomas Andrews found, as he only made minor adjustments to the heating of some cabins. The ship also leaned slightly on the port side because of the poor balancing of coal stocks, but this had no effect on the ship. Over the next few days, the weather was glorious. The sun was in the sky from morning to night in a perfectly blue sky. The sea was calm and the wind was light, allowing passengers to take long walks on the deck.

However, the beautiful weather, however pleasant for the passengers, was far more problematic for the marine pilots. The mild winter in the far north had detached large expanses of ice in Greenland. On the other hand, colder temperatures in the south prevented them from melting. It was therefore a true sea of icebergs that loomed ahead of the *Titanic* and warnings quickly arrived, directing the ship away from the presence of ice between 46° and 41°30' north latitude and 51° to 40°40' west longitude. Ignoring these warnings, the captain carried on full steam ahead.

On Sunday 14 April, the day, which was as beautiful as those before it, began with a church service officiated by the captain himself for the first-class passengers, then proceeded as usual, the only exception being that the temperature was slightly lower. As a result, the passengers did not enjoy the ship's lounges as much as they had the previous few days. However, in the telegraph room, the atmosphere was different. Since 9am, the operators had been receiving more warnings about the presence of icebergs. No fewer than seven messages were received during the day, the last of which arrived at 11pm. However, due to the lack of time and the absence of the main officers scattered throughout the ship, only one of these messages reached the commander, who was at a dinner prepared in his honor, and to the pilot. Thus, nearly all of the officers on guard were unaware that the *Titanic* was headed for an ice zone at a speed of 22.5 knots.

Certainly, the sea was crystal clear on 14 April, which comforted the captain in his belief that any iceberg would be quickly spotted. But, on a moonless night without wind or waves to make the ice bounce, what happened was just the opposite. In their 15 meter high tower, the two lookouts surveyed the horizon in temperatures of 0 °C. At 11:40pm, they froze: an increasingly large dark mass was appearing in the distance. They immediately rang the bell and phoned the bridge shouting "Iceberg, right ahead!". The first officer, William Murdoch (1873-1912), immediately ordered the man at the helm to steer towards the port side, before communicating to the engine room to immediately stop the ship and put the engines in reverse. Despite the quick orders, the ship was too big in relation to its rudder to turn quickly: the impact with the iceberg spotted 450 meters away seemed inevitable. Although the top of the *Titanic* avoided the obstacle, the bottom of the hull was not so lucky. For nearly 90 meters, the ship scraped the submerged part of the iceberg. Under the pressure of the shock, the metal sheets were twisted and blew the rivets. There were now six holes in the bottom of the *Titanic*.

WOMEN AND CHILDREN FIRST

While the iceberg was still scraping along the hull, Officer William Murdoch immediately activated the closing of the watertight doors of the hull. Captain Edward John Smith also left his cabin and sent men to inspect the damage before heading to the ship's lower deck himself, accompanied by Thomas Andrews. For most passengers, the crash went unnoticed; the most they felt was a slight jerk. The situation was much worse in the lower decks. The first five compartments of the *Titanic* and boiler room no. 6 were affected by the impact. Water poured into the compartments, submerging the mechanics, who had only a few seconds to evacuate once the door closing switch was activated.

Faced with this disaster, Thomas Andrews was the first to realize the fate that now awaited the *Titanic*. The ship had been built to be able to stay afloat with four compartments flooded. Yet there were five compartments that had been flooded. The watertight doors beyond the fourth compartment went no higher than Deck E (the last level before the engine room) and water would simply pass over the walls, inexorably submerging one compartment after another. The architect, aware of the human catastrophe that would ensue, announced to the captain that the ship he believed to be unsinkable was about to sink. According to his estimates, the sea giant had only one hour, maybe two, left.

The captain made quick decisions. He first asked the mechanics to evacuate the steam boilers to prevent explosions, while maintaining enough pressure to keep the electricity running. He then gathered the crew to prepare lifeboats and gather the passengers on the deck. At the telegraph station, he finally asked the operators to immediately send distress signals to all vessels in the vicinity. The message "MGY [indicative of the *Titanic*] CQD CQD [Come Quickly Distress]. Come immediately. We have struck a berg. Position 41.44 N 50.24 W" (Masson 1998, p. 49) was sent dozens of times. The *Carpathia* was the first to come to the rescue of the *Titanic*, but it did not arrive until 4am. However, another ship's lights could be seen in the distance, but the ghost ship – probably a smuggling ship – did not react to the calls the distress signals of the *Titanic*. Vanishing into the night, the ship left the liner in the hands of fate.

For the passengers, confusion ensued. Very few had seen the iceberg and everyone felt safe in the safest liner in the world. The staff had also had no real training for the evacuation of the ship. However, gradually, the passengers gathered on the deck, starting with those in first class, in the infernal din of steam whistling through the chimneys. At 12:25am, when the ship began to lean forward, the captain ordered the boarding of the lifeboats. As was customary, it was mainly women and children who were called first, even though, in reality, some men would also be able to board them.

In the mayhem, many mistakes were made. The boats, with a capacity of 65 adults, were filled to only half or less. At 12:45am, the first set off with only 28 passengers on board. Gradually, as time passed, the other passengers began to understand in amazement what was happening and gave in to panic. In the telegraph cabin, the operators decided to send another distress signal, the first SOS (Save Our Souls) in history. Understanding the urgency of the situation, some passengers became true heroes, such as the gentlemen who spent their last moments trying to save as many women and children as possible, or the men of the orchestra, who tried to soothe the last moments of the hundreds of people who were trapped on the *Titanic*.

THE DISAPPEARANCE OF THE TITAN

At 1:45am, the 16 lifeboats of the *Titanic* had been sent out to sea and gradually sailed away from the vessel. There were only four collapsible boats left. Only two were sent out: Collapsible Boat C, at 1:45am, and Collapsible Boat D, at 2:05am. The other two fell overboard, as a result of the ever stronger leaning of the ship, and sailed adrift, saving several swimmers. Panic then reached its peak on board, which threatened the descent of the last boats. The officers were forced to restore order under the threat of guns. After the departure of the last boat, the commander freed his crew so that everyone could try to save their lives. However, many remained at their post, including the two radio operators who, at 2:17am, with water at their feet, sent the last SOS call of the *Titanic*.

Collapsible boat transporting the last survivors of the Titanic, April 1912.

Meanwhile, for the passengers in the lifeboats, the sight was indescribable. With the stern propellers now out of the water and making a deafening noise, everything onboard the *Titanic* slid forward. At 2:17am, when the stern was raised to about 45°, the lights began to flash before shutting down permanently, after which the first two chimneys collapsed in turn. Seconds later, under the extreme pressure engendered by the sinking of the hull, the world's largest passenger ship split in two, between the third and fourth chimney, with a deafening sound. The bow then began its long descent into the abyss, while the stern, raised vertically, sank in turn. At 2:20am, the plate engraved with the name of the *Titanic* disappeared into the ocean.

The Titanic sinking, 1912.

Hundreds of passengers were sucked down to the seabed along with the liner. For the others, the ordeal was far from over. Screaming for help, they found themselves swimming in -2 °C water, forced to suffer a slow agony. Among the survivors in the boats, the fear of capsizing outweighed the wish to help others. Only one collapsible boat returned in search of survivors after more than an hour of waiting. Among the hundreds of bodies, four people were hauled out of the water. Finally, at around 4am, the lights of the *Carpathia* appeared to the last survivors. It was not until 8am that the last 10 survivors boarded the ship. The tragedy was colossal: of the 2 200 onboard the *Titanic*, only 700 survived.

REPERCUSSIONS

ENHANCED SECURITY

On both sides of the Atlantic, the tragedy of the *Titanic* caused quite a stir. From 19 April 1912, the day after the arrival of the survivors onboard the *Carpathia*, a US investigation committee looked into the disaster. This was followed some weeks later by an inquiry of the British Board of Trade, the committee responsible for the legislation on maritime trade.

The US commission would prove more severe than the British committee regarding the owners of the ship, blaming Joseph Bruce Ismay, among others, for having survived when so many others perished. However, the two investigations arrived at relatively similar conclusions. Although the design of the *Titanic* was not called into question, the idea of an unsinkable boat was banished forever. In addition, it was recognized that the ship did not have a sufficient number of rescue boats and that, moreover, it was traveling too fast. However, the lack of lifeboats did not breach legislation, and Captain Smith was exonerated of charges of negligence. The commission nevertheless found a scapegoat in Stanley Lord (1877-1962), captain of the *Californian*. At the time, everyone thought that his boat was the ghost ship which ignored the distress calls of the *Titanic*. However, after the discovery of the position of the wreck, the discredited captain was rehabilitated, long after his death.

In light of the disaster, nations and shipping companies

learned the necessary lessons. The authorities required the establishment of new safety regulations for shipping. The transatlantic routes were changed: ships would henceforth go further south to avoid drifting ice. Furthermore, they would now have a sufficient number of lifeboats to carry all the passengers and crew members. Similarly, when traveling, commanders would be required to conduct rescue and evacuation drills so that everyone would be prepared in the case of an emergency. Finally, telegraphs and radio would now be mandatory, with operators present 24 hours a day for vessels with a capacity of over 50 people.

The sinking of the *Titanic* also resulted in the organization of several conferences on safety at sea. At the end of 1913, the main countries dependent on shipping in the North Atlantic agreed to create the International Ice patrol. The organization, operational since 1912 on the initiative of the US Navy, is responsible for patrolling and monitoring advanced ice and drifting icebergs in the Northwest Atlantic. If applicable, vessels located in the sector were informed and deflected by the patrol to avoid any accidents. Still active today with means such as aircrafts, the International Ice Patrol brings together 17 countries. The success of the organization has been total. To date, no further accidents have been caused by a collision with an iceberg floating in the Northwest Atlantic.

THE BIRTH OF A MYTH

The *Titanic* tragedy was so imprinted in collective memories that is still strikes the imagination today. In 1912, the press was the first to seize the news of the shipwreck. For days, the ship made the headlines, each reporter giving his explanation for the accident, the list of missing or saved passengers, as well as the first testimonies of the survivors. This press coverage was followed by literature and film. Soon after the tragedy, the first books written by the survivors were published. To date, there are no fewer than 850 books dedicated to the *Titanic*, reflecting the incredible success of its story.

Meanwhile, more than a dozen films chronicling the final hours of the giant liner, not to mention documentaries, have been released. The first came out barely a month after the tragedy, on 14 May 1912, causing outrage amongst the traumatized survivors. A few years later, the *Titanic* even became the subject of Nazi propaganda, when Joseph Goebbels (German politician, 1897-1945) claimed that a German had been the true hero of the sinking, stating that he saved several lives, unlike the British, who he alleged were responsible for the tragedy. However, the film that achieved the most resounding success was James Cameron's (born in 1954), which revived the popularity of the disappeared ship in 1997.

Besides history, the *Titanic* has also been the object of fantasy. From the first years following the tragedy, several companies dreamed of refloating the vessel, as the investigation committees had claimed that it had sunk whole. However, the lack of technological resources at the time meant that each attempt led to failure. It was not until the 1980s that the wreck was finally identified. In 1985,

American geologist Robert Ballard (born in 1942), of the Woods Hole Oceanographic institution, launched a search for the *Titanic*. In order to stack the odds in his favor, he developed an underwater exploration device, named Argo, equipped with cameras, and a small remote-controlled robot called Jason. The research ship even had a lateral sonar. After more than a month and a half searching a surface of 250 km^2, on 1 September 1985, Argo transmitted the images of the wreck. There was no doubt that it was the *Titanic*. In the days that followed, the researchers discovered that the bow and the stern of the ship are separated by 600 meters of debris, calling into question the conclusions of the investigations: the ship had indeed broken during the sinking. The next year, a new expedition set out with researchers in submarines. For the first time since the tragedy, men were able to see the liner up close. Since then, dozens of expeditions have taken places, bringing thousands of objects to the surface, from simple pieces of coal to a huge metal plate from the hull.

Today, the wreck of the *Titanic* is on the verge of disappearing, eaten away by the sea and the currents, but the splendor of the ship, which aroused such admiration during its time will, along with its story, remain forever etched in our memories.

View of the bow of the wreck of the Titanic, June 2004.

SUMMARY

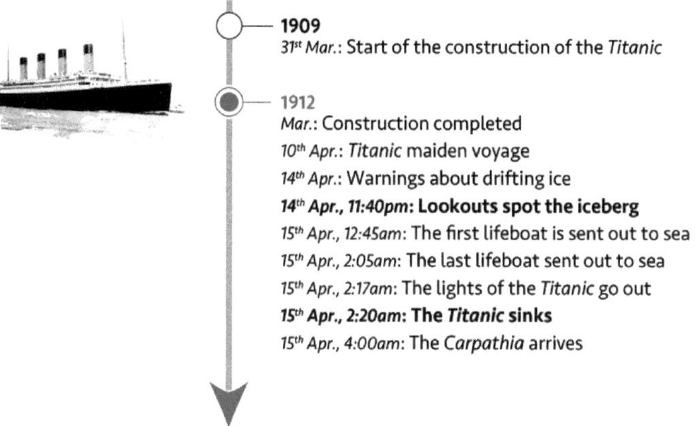

- In order to compete with the *Mauretania* and *Lusitania* ships of the Cunard Line company, Joseph Bruce Ismay, chairman of the White Star Line, launched a project in 1907 to build three giant ships, one of which would be the *Titanic*.

- The construction of the giant vessel began on 31 March 1909 in the Harland & Wolff shipyards in Belfast. The work was completed three years later, in March 1912, making the *Titanic* liner the largest, grandest and most luxurious in the world.

- The maiden voyage of the *Titanic* began on 10 April 1912 from Southampton. The ship narrowly avoided a collision with the *New York*, whose moorings were broken. It then went to Cherbourg and Queenstown to board the last passengers before crossing the Atlantic.

- At 1:30pm on 11 April, the *Titanic* departed from the coast of Ireland to New York. The weather was glorious during the first three days.
- However, to the west, the situation looked more problematic due to the presence of icebergs.
- On Sunday 14 April, warnings about drifting ice in the *Titanic*'s path began to intensify. However, the captain maintained the ship's speed and believed he could avoid the danger.
- Nonetheless, due to poor visibility conditions, the lookouts noticed the iceberg too later at 11:40pm.
- Immediately informed, the officer on duty diverted the ship, and ordered the engines to be halted and put in reverse. But the *Titanic*, due to its weight, reacted too slowly. The starboard side of the hull scraped the submerged iceberg. The pressure caused the opening of several holes.
- Captain Smith and the architect Thomas Andrews then discovered the severity of the damage. Five compartments of the ship were affected, while the ship could only withstand four flooded compartments: the *Titanic* was doomed. While there were 2 200 people onboard, only 1 178 seats were available in the lifeboats.
- An evacuation was immediately ordered and distress signals were sent to all the nearby ships. At 12:45am, the first lifeboat was sent out to sea. The last one touched the water at 2:05am. Meanwhile, the vessel was leaning further and further forward, until it reached an angle of 45°.
- At 2:17am, the *Titanic*'s lights flickered and eventually went out permanently. The first two chimneys collapsed,

crushing dozens of people. Finally, under the colossal pressure of the sinking, the ship broke in two, between the third and fourth chimneys. The bow sank as the stern reached a vertical position, before plunging to the depths of the ocean at 2:20am.

- The hundreds of passengers that were still onboard were then sucked into the sea with the wreck or threw themselves into the icy water with nobody coming to their aid. Among the dead, only four people were rescued from the water alive, after waiting for over an hour.
- Coming to the rescue of the *Titanic*, the *Carpathia* arrived at around 4am. It was not until 8:10am that the last survivor boarded the vessel.

We want to hear from you!
Leave a comment on your online library
and share your favourite books on social media!

FIND OUT MORE

BIBLIOGRAPHY

* Béchu, J.-P. (1980) *La Belle Époque et son envers. Quand la caricature écrit l'histoire.* Monte-Carlo: Sauret.
* Howells, R.P. (1999) *The Myth of the Titanic.* New York: St. Martin's Press.
* *Les paquebots. Histoire d'un siècle. 1843–1944* (1987) Paris: Le Livre de Paris.
* Masson, P. (1998) *Le Titanic.* Paris: Tallandier.
* Peillard, L. (1972) *Sur les chemins de l'océan. Paquebots 1830–1972.* Paris: Hachette.
* Pierre, M. (1999) *1900/1910. Une presque Belle Époque.* Paris: Gallimard.
* Riffenburgh, B. (2012) *Titanic: The Legend of the Unsinkable Ship.* London: André Deutsch.

ADDITIONAL SOURCES

* Eaton, J.P. and Haas, C.A. (1998) *Titanic: Triumph and Tragedy.* New York/London: Patrick Stephens.
* Freeman, H. (2016) *Titanic: The Story About the Unsinkable Ship.* CreateSpace Independent Publishing Platform.
* Hutchings, D. (2008) *The Titanic Story.* Stroud, Gloucestershire: The History Press.
* Lord, W. (2012) *A Night to Remember: The Classic Bestselling Account of the Sinking of the Titanic.* London: Penguin.
* Mayo, J. (2016) *Titanic: Minute By Minute.* London: Short

Books Ltd.

ICONOGRAPHIC SOURCES

- Thomas Edison and his photographer, 1878. © Levin C. Handy.
- Ford Model T, 1910. © Harry Shipler.
- Edward John Smith, 1912. Royalty-free reproduction picture.
- Joseph Bruce Ismay, 1912. Royalty-free reproduction picture.
- Titanic's departure from Southampton, 10 April 1912. © Francis Godolphin Osbourne Stuart.
- Collapsible boat transporting the last survivors of the Titanic, April 1912. The photo was taken by one of the passengers of the *Carpathia*, the ship that answered the SOS call of the Titanic. Royalty-free reproduction picture.
- Titanic sinking, 1912. © Willy Stöwer.
- View of the bow of the wreck of the Titanic, June 2004. Royalty-free reproduction picture.

FILMS AND DOCUMENTARIES

- *A Night to Remember.* (1958) [Film]. Roy Ward Baker. Dir. UK: The Rank Organisation.
- *Titanic.* (1997) [Film]. James Cameron. Dir. USA: 20th Century Fox, Paramount Pictures, Lightstorm Entertainment.
- *Ghosts of the Abyss.* (2003) [Documentary]. James Cameron. Dir. USA: Walt Disney Pictures.

- *Titanic: Blood and Steel.* (2012) [Television Series]. Ciaran
  Donnelly. Dir. Ireland: De Angelis Group.
- *Titanic : l'Ultime Scénario.* (2012) [Documentary]. Herlé
  Jouon. Dir. France: Grand Angle Productions.

MUSEUMS AND COMMEMORATIVE MONUMENTS

- Harland & Wolff shipyards (Ireland).
- *Titanic* shipwreck (North Atlantic, 41° 43' 57''N;
  49°56'49''O).
- Commemorative monument of the *Titanic*, Belfast
  (Ireland).
- Commemorative monument of the *Titanic*, New York
  (United States).
- Titanic museum, Belfast (Northern Ireland).
- Titanic museum, Indian Orchard, Massachusetts (United
  States).

IMPROVE YOUR GENERAL KNOWLEDGE

IN A BLINK OF AN EYE !

www.50minutes.com

www.50minutes.com

Ebook EAN: 9782806276025

Paperback EAN: 9782806276650

Legal Deposit: D/2016/12603/60

Cover: © Primento

Digital conception by Primento, the digital partner of publishers.